"Life's Reflections"

A journey towards acceptance.
An eclectic weave of poetry, nature
and Reflection.
Connecting with people along the way,
And the amazing power of prayer.

BY
Nancy T. Kirkwood

ISBN: 13 978-1727658569
ISBN: 10 1727658566

Dedication

This book is dedicated to:
my best friend and husband Richard.
When I count my blessings
I count him twice!

To our children and their spouses
Kevin & Mia
Joseph
Bonnie & Frank
Colleen & Vince
and
Katie & Hiten

To our grandchildren
Elizabeth, Mike, Claire, Megan,
Michelle, Frank, Ryan,
Marina and Gavin

My family is my joy and my inspiration!

ACKNOWLEDGEMENTS

Our personalities are shaped & influenced
by many factors and experiences but it is the
people in our lives who make a difference.
FAITH - FAMILY - FRIENDS

I am grateful for my parents who planted
the seeds of Faith and taught by example.
I am grateful for the teamwork of my family
Lead by my daughter-in-law in helping to
publish this book
I am grateful for my husband's encouragement
and the poem he wrote that you will find on page 35.
I am grateful for the bond that exits with my siblings.
I am grateful for the friends that I have known
at every stage of my life. From the friend I met in
kindergarten to the new friends I have met after I was
diagnosed with Parkinson's
and all those in-between. My life has been
enriched by friends and so the first poem of my
book is for all of you my dear friends old and new.
The poem is simply called
FRIEND.

TABLE OF CONTENTS #1

TABLE OF CONTENTS # 2

TABLE OF CONTENTS #3

Life is a Journey

Take a walk with me on a path that brings you through my perennial, butterfly and Signature Gardens.

I'll mix in my poems about everyday situations for which I a hope you can relate. I will share my reflections and some of my story counting my blessings along the way.

I invite you to do the same. We all have a story, a journey in life and when we connect we become kindred spirits.

Try to be present in he moment, engaged in life for that is where God shows His face. Look for the spirit filled moments. If you are seeking you will find them.

Life is a journey and we lift one another up when we connect and genuinely care. When we embrace life completely, we take the good and the bad and we make soup out of the ingredients that we've been given. Our life is enriched by people connecting with people.

The best flavor in soup comes from making good use of the brown bits. That extra step makes a difference! The dance of life must be lived one day at a time.

Why not live with passion and love? We grow and learn from our mistakes, we never walk alone! God is with us in all the joys and celebrations in life. He is also with us in pain, loneliness, and all of the messy bits in between.

Our Creator loves us just as we are.

He calls us all by name.
We are His hands and feet!

Listen and respond.

A friend feeds the soul

A friend is a treasure

A friend is a gift.

POEM 1

Friend

A Friend is a treasure,
A special gift.

A friend is right there
If you need a lift.

A friend accepts you
Just as you are.

You stay close wherever you live,
No matter how far.

A friend challenges you to be
The best you can be.

How lucky I am to have a
Friend like thee.

My life could be compared to a Perennial

Garden, ever changing and filled with colorful adventures. I have known many interesting people who have made a difference. I think that God has planted all of us in the place that we are meant to be.

My husband and I enjoyed the busy years while our children were growing up. Looking back there are so many memories that live in a mother's heart. Each stage in a child's growth and development has its joys and a measure of challenges. I choose to never forget the good things. The laughter, the tender hugs, the giggles, the jokes, the milestones, and challenges faced and resolved. I recall the sparkle in their eyes when they were happy and *I saw God's love shining within.* Now that they are grown I pray that I was able to plant the seeds of Faith in their hearts as my parents did. There is great joy in being a Grandparent it is the circle of life and always a privilege when we can get together and spend time as a family. I am grateful when our children share their children with my husband and I for a child is twice blessed if they have grow up being loved not only by their parents but also by their Grandparents and Aunts & Uncles and cousins. The perennial garden produces beautiful flowers when weeded and the soil nourished and cared for by the Gardner. **There is no replacement for the time spent together with family.**

The Grandparent Connection

My Dad's parents lived close to my grade school.

Every Wednesday the grandchildren would go for lunch.
My Grandma always made it special. Sometimes she
would have a" theme" like **Hot dog Boats and root
beer floats.** Sometimes we would have pancakes,
Or a formal lunch in the dining room with extra plates
and a lesson on manners and which was your bread plate
and water glass. She always made a fuss and we
knew we were loved. My joy in entertaining and
planning theme parties through the years comes
from those memories of Wednesday lunches. If there
was a "party gene" mine came from my Grandma!
My fondest memory is the **TEA PARTY** my Grandma
gave me for my 8th grade graduation gift. It was just for
my Mom and I and we were told to dress up and wear a
hat because it would be outside. The magic began for me
just as we walked into her back yard. Grandpa had
moved the table right in the middle of the yard next to
her **Perennial garden in full bloom.** The sky was a crisp
blue, the Spring grass green and the table was set with a
white lace tablecloth and china dishes and the site took
my breath away! It was like walking into Alice and
Wonderland. Grandpa was the waiter and he was
wearing a suit. At the end of our lunch I was given my
first Journal

My Mom's Mom died when I was ten. I have
a fond memory of staying overnight with my
cousin and sleeping on her Murphy bed that pulled
out from the wall and walking to Church in the
morning. My Grandpa died of TB when my Mom
was a baby so she never knew her Dad.
I was lucky to have known 3 Grandparents!

*O*ur *family has many traditions.*

Here are some of our family's best.

Christmas Pageant

This tradition began in 1972 with four cousins at my
parents's house. We now have dozens of cousins and a
multitude of angels. The costumes have expanded as the
family grew.
The ***Christmas Story*** is read by the older cousins and
parents. The children in costumes beam with delight.
This begins Christmas for me! The seeds of faith are
planted, a garden matures in time.

The year 2000

New Century - A New Tradition

The **Letters Party** began in 2000. Instead of buying something from a store for Christmas, we asked our children to write down a family memory and share it at a letters party. They were encouraged to "pay it forward" by donating to a charity or doing a secret act of kindness. Every year the letters are a special gift. The best part is that the letters are read out loud and shared with the group.

If someone cannot come we use technology with face time face time so everyone is included. Our family history is being written in real time by our family and the letters are more than a gift, they are a treasure! The grandchildren have started to make a contribution which is a good sign that the tradition has taken off and is likely to continue.

The letters are laminated and kept in 3-ring binders and placed under the Christmas Tree. During the holidays when visiting the family can read notes from past years. This was my husband's idea and just recently the grandkids are starting to write a note Which is a good sign that the tradition is likely to continue.

Treasure Hunts with the Grand kids

We often have treasure Hunts with our Grandkids. We have multi-colored bandanas and the kids choose their color and put them on "pirate style". Papa has one walkie talkie and the kids share the other. Papa first asks for the "Pirates call - ARR!" They have to walk the plank, the plank is a 2x4 that papa has sanded and sealed and for the big kids it is easy but for the little ones it is not and they all try and the bigger cousins help. Papa has the kids running and hopping on one foot, doing the chicken dance and all kinds of silly fun and eventually they find the treasure and it's divided among the pirates.
GREAT FUN FOR ALL!

Paying it Forward

Years ago, I was grocery shopping with two small children in one cart and pulling another with my food and some stranger bought my groceries! When I went to pay I was I was given a note that read : **"You can thank me by doing an act of kindness for someone else".** Since then I have tried to find ways to pay it forward. I recalled the different ways my mom had taught the lesson and made it fun.She would bake multiple lamb cakes at Easter time. I would help frost them and add coconut and then Mom would include Me in the decision of who might enjoy this Easter treat giving me a couple? We always had fun delivering them because they were so cute.
Mom gave the mold when my children were young and we did the same. I recall one year our list was big so we made 7 lambs and when they were lined up on my table and my husband said it looked like a herd. It was a funny site decorating the herd with frosting and coconut all over but it was fun. We only did that many one year!

My Mom had a way of just being there for people and I once asked her how knew who might need a visit or a word of encouragement?
Her answer was simply prayer.
We guess, Jesus knows - ASK HIM!

Learning by Example

Children learn best if they are taught by the

Example set for them and I learned from the best!
My parents kept their relationship a priority by having Date
Nights. My Mom use to say that many hands make light the
work. Every family member had certain responsibilities according
to our ages and we were expected to do our chores. They never
expected perfection but encouraged us to always give our best.
They treated others with kindness and expected us to do the same.
They gave us responsibilities and the freedom to make mistakes
and learn from them. Our home was always a safe place and I was
one of 8 children and all of us felt loved. My parents had couple
friends and they had individual friends. They worked
hard and taught us all a good work ethic. Education was important. We ate our meals together and we went to Church together.
My husband and I tried to teach our children in the same way &
we also had date nights and when money was tight sometimes it
was just taking a long walk together. Now that Our children are
grown I am always proud to see our children are instilling good
values, building memories and teaching by their example. When I
Nana hears the Grandkids giggle and say their parents are on a
date it makes me smile knowing that my children are
keeping their relationship a priority. I pray that that I have done
my job and planted the seeds of faith as my parents did for me and
that they plant seeds for their children because in the end
What is important are God's commands to HAVE FAITH, HOPE
and LOVE and the greatest is LOVE!

Nancy Kirkwood 17

Take the time to scatter seeds

The Seed

A simple deed - a little deed
A moment shared,
A life enriched because someone
Stopped, and really cared.

It only takes a little extra
Effort to encourage and plant a
Seed, to fill a void, a need.

That little seed can reach further than
You may think.
Plants will flourish with sunshine and
Just a little drink.

Sometimes we think that only the big
Things we do are grand, when
Heartfelt giving can be as simple as
Holding out your hand.

So, as you walk the path of life,
Scatter many seeds of hope and love.
Don't worry if the seeds will grow,
Leave that job to the one above!

MY SIGNATURE GARDEN

This Garden tells a story

Every Garden Tells A Story

This garden connects five generations of family.

44 first names written on moon shaped stones that fit together to make a K for our last name, Kirkwood. This is my Signature Garden. The K is completed with a walking path made of recycled tires painted with family vacations in a quilt like pattern. Each square has a story to tell. The pathway continues behind the shed into a "secret garden" with daisies and sunflowers. And day lilies.I created this garden while my husband was doing research on his ancestry. A 12-year search led him to a patriot soldier who fought with George Washington. My husband loves history and finding a direct descendant who served in the Revolutionary war, gave him a renewed sense of pride in his own service in the Vietnam era and a connection to generations that came before. He is in the process of writing down his research for our family history to be kept with the family letters.

Every person has a Unique story. What is your story?

INTRODUCTION TO POETRY

My first introduction to poetry came in 8th grade when we had an assignment to memorize the poem Trees by Kilmore. I was fascinated with the emotion behind the words that were simple but had a profound meaning. I wanted to able to write poems some day!

I went to the library and started reading poetry books which opened a whole new world for me. Each Author had their own style but they all had the ability to captivate and bring to the "word" an element that just drew me in. I had no idea how they did it but I was inspired to try to write poetry. I started by writing down my thoughts and would go back to at a latr time and make up little poems.

Within walking distance to my house was a little Snack Shop run by an outgoing, fun loving widow . Her customers were all local people who lived or worked in town. I started working there as a Freshman and worked there all through my High School Years. I would bring in my poems for my Boss to critique. It was a fun place to work and my Boss was a Mentor a Friend and a Gift to my life.

The Cornell Snack Shop will always hold a special place in my heart because I met my husband there.

POETRY READING

The summer after my Freshman year one of the customer's told me about a place in town where local Actors were reading poetry and they had an open mike once a week for inspiring poets. That summer I went every week and read my poems and listened to other people's poems which were better than mine. The place was very low key. They had a coffee pot in the back with a sign to bring your own mug and a stage with fording chairs. No food was served but people sometimes brought in brownies or cookies I never had any coffee or ate anything because my Boss had warned me to NEVER eat or drink at any establishment because sometimes drugs were being added and it was best just to say no. That was excellent advice and I embellished it.

There was no official judging of poems, it was all audience driven. Cheers and loud clapping would get a 2nd chance to read your poem which meant the audience approved. I had read several poems on different nights and just received a polite clap which wasn't good enough. My goal was to get that 2nd call and I knew I would have to step it up in order to be recognized. I started writing a poem I called **UNIQUE.** When it was completed I knew it was better but wasn't sure if it was good enough. I practiced my delivery and I wore my favorite summer outfit - Orange pedal pushers and a top with a sunflower. (Pedal pushers were the 60's version of capris). I had nothing to lose, no teacher to judge, just a personal goal, a summer experience and the best I could do! I confidently walked up to the stage even thou my stomach was churning inside and I read my poem **'UNIQUE'** **and to my utter amazement the entire audience of about 20 people stood up clapping and cheering you did it! I couldn't believe it and I was over the moon with joy!** I thanked God and remembered that day in the library when I had hoped to someday find the words that would reach people's hearts. **It was a small group of people sitting on folding chairs and I was THE KID but at least for that moment in time my words had connected. Praise God!**

CELEBRATING F0R
DIFFERENT REASONS

My parents shared in my celebration but little did I know that they were waiting for me to reach my goal because they wanted that to be my exit to leave the older audience behind.. Unfortunately for my parents, my victory only fueled the fire and I was even more committed. Since their **"wait and see strategy"** didn't work that had to make that "tough love" move to protect their oldest daughter. I had finished my homework and was chilling with the music on my little transistor radio with the the ear plugs enjoying the fact that my younger sister was at a sleepover and I had the room to myself. My Mom knocked on my door and asked me to come in the kitchen for a minute. I had no clue what this was about but I sensed that it wasn't good news. My Mom started by saying that they were proud that I had set a goal and wrote a poem that got a standing ovation but she & my Dad felt it was a good time to leave the older audience behind. Perhaps I would like to get a group of teens together and they could meet in our basement ? Then my Dad spoke, he was a WW2 Veteran and received a bronze star in The Battle of the Bulge. He was not in favor of our involvement in SE Asia but he also did want me getting caught up in the melting pot of an emerging counter culture known to be present in places like little coffee houses. It just wasn't a suitable place for his teenage daughter. I PLEAED MY CASE and protested that it was just one night a week, I wasn't dating anyone & I was home by 10:30. There was just 3 more times before school started and I begged to be able to go 3 more times. **My dad was firm and said that he and Mom had decided its was best for me and the answer was NO. I was furious and went back to my room slamming the door as hard as I could!**

LOST POEMS

I was angry and felt that my parents were being unreasonable. They had supported me all along and now that I finally achieved my goal they turned on me? Why couldn't I go just 3 more times, what harm could that be? I had never been at such odds with my parents before and that made me sad, but I felt they got this one wrong. I am sure my hormones were not helping matters but the intensity of the moment made for irrational actions on my part. I went to my mattress and pulled out all of my notes and my boxes of finished poems and started to rip them up piece by piece until the room was covered with shredded paper. I was emotionally drained and physically exhausted and just went to sleep with puffy eyes and tears rolling down my cheeks. The next morning I woke up to my room filled with shreds of paper. I was faced with the reality that my own impulsive actions had done this. The remorse I felt in my gut was horrible. There was no cloud, no There was no USB, no remote hard drive, no dropbox. My poems were Lost forever and I had only myself to blame. I had to get the room cleaned before my sister came home. I made my bed and started collecting all he pieces of paper filling a large garbage bag. I took the bag out behind the garage where we had a burn barrel and dumped the paper in. **And watched in disbelief how in a split second years of my creative expression was reduced to CARBON-WATER AND HEAT.**
I convinced myself that most of the poems weren't that good anyway but I was very sorry that I had destroyed "Unique" because that one was good. I thought that maybe I could re-write it but for what use. **It was the end of my Adolescent Poetry Phase and I didn't write again for many years.**

(Please note that in the 60's everyone burned paper and we didn't recycle either. I am so glad that we have progressed to a place where at least we have started to care about the environment.).

Parkinson's Diagnosed

Time marches on and our family was growing. Three of our children were married, and we had 7 grandchildren, We had one adult son at home & working full-time and our youngest daughter was in College. The high energy days with a house full of young children had passed and so when health issues surfaced the timing was much better than if we had a young family. For about 5 years prior to my diagnosis I was noticing changes in the way I walked and I would call it Nana's giddy up. I was having balance issues so I was going to Tai Chi twice a week My sense of smell was going away and I first discovered while camping when the family all smelled skunk, but I didn't. Apparently it was pretty obvious and the kids kept repeating, really Mom you can't smell that? I thought that was a good thing but did miss the smell of coffee and my roses & the turkey roasting on Thanksgiving. My other other senses were sharper and that seemed to more than justify the loss of smell. I once had a beautiful handwriting and did calligraphy but now letters that I mailed started coming back. I now print and consciously force myself to right Big. There were other changes, stiffness and my left side was weaker and my left foot would drag unexpectedly and causing a number of falls. One landed me down the stairs and in the hospital w/ 5 herniated discs. Parkinson's was certainly there but not diagnosed yet.. One day when walking the Mall and I noticed that my left arm did not swing when I walked and I I remembered that as being a question on my Nursing Boards as a sign of Parkinson's. I made an appointment with a Neurologist.

The very next day I was serving a Funeral Lunch at my Church and my Aunt and Uncle were at thatlunch. (This was not an accident) My Uncle had Parkinson's and was at the end stage of the disease. After they finished their lunch I sat down we talked. The next day my entire extended family knew and my Uncle called apologizing for spilling the beans but said he had asked the family to pray for me to make things easier. Our family is like an army and you need to use the Army who lovesyou! We bonded with that and prayed for one another. I shared my poems and the desire to publish. **My Uncle was a gift to his family but he was aso a gift to me!**

The road to acceptance is a process -
A balance of letting go & asking for God's help.

I am a Registered Nurse and after I was diagnosed
I wanted to know everything new that was being done so my
husband and I went to seminars, read articles did research at
the library and internet searches the knowledge initially was
a good thing but at some point I became overwhelmed and
depressed. The one good thing that came out of this phase
was that I found a new doctor who was Neurologist but also
a Movement Specialist. She is a genuine and kind person
besides being knowledgeable and she stayed after her semi-
nar to talk with me even though she had a family waiting at
home. **My new Doctor was another gift that came to me
along my journey!**
Whenever you come to place in your life when you
have a start a new journey and walk the road less traveled
you have to accept what you cannot change! I was having
trouble doing this. I was resistant to all the changes, the
walker, the canes, my slowness. I was struggling and not accepting until finally I did what I should have done in the beginning and that was to **ASK FOR GOD'S HELP!** I don't
know why it took me so long, but even coming in desperation
as soon as I asked and opened the door,
HE WAS THERE filling my restlesss soul with **PEACE!**
I knew that I would be OK, the Shepherd would guide me.

Early the next day I found myself writing down my thoughts and they were coming in poetic form just as they had as a teenager. Could it be that God had given back to me something I had thrown away so many years ago? Before the sun came up I had written the poem **THE MESSY BITS OF LIFE**. It was to be another Gift that I would received on journey with Parkinson's. I laminated multiple copies and started to give this poem away because **gifts are meant to be shared.** This poem was reaching people's hearts in ways that I never would have expected. This poem was the driving force that set me on a path to publish.

This is the 3rd poem in my book.

Its placement is to honor the Trinity.

The Messy Bits of Life

is all about the Messy Bits,
The hard choices, the challenges, the
Struggles and the life changing events
That with you remain.

The sanctuary is found in acceptance,
Letting go,
Making the necessary changes,
Taking control,
and staying in the game.

There is joy and abundant strength
That emerges when you walk the road
Less traveled.

The path meant for you is
Placed on steady ground.

When dealing with the messy bits it's
All about love!
Love opens the door and conquers fear.

God will embrace you and fill the
Empty space.

All that really matters is how much we have loved.

Nancy Kirkwood **29**

MUSIC and DANCE REPLACES POETRY

Music and dance have been part of my life as far back as I can remember. As a little girl I got the nickname Nance because I loved to dance.

I took Irish dance lessons in grade school and competed in local competitions. In Junior High my friends and I tuned into **American bandstand and danced along with the TV kids** and learned all the moves to the twist, the cha cha, the mashed potato, the Freddie, the Hitch-Hiker, the Shimmy, the Swim, the Monkey, the Boogaloo, the Jerk and a whole lot more! I danced and sang in 2 High School Musicals and danced a jig in a little show we had in Nursing School and at every Wedding when a jig was played. **I was watching the Ed Sullivan Show on a tiny TV screen when the Beatles** came to America and like all the girls I had my favorite Beatle and was caught up in Beatle mania. I have always gone to music as an outlet of pure joy! Recently my husband and I started to reflect and rekindle the memories of our youth, our courtship and the music that we loved. Inspired by Michael J. Fox we called it the **"way back machine"** and it brought **"Sugar & Spice"** to our marriage. *I thank God everyday for sending my husband into my life. We have walked together down many a winding road and hit the back roads together and always got to the main road with the help of the Shepherd and now we were heading into a new adventure.*

Sugar & Spice was the title of one of the songs from a local garage band called the Cryan' Shames. They were the House band for a Teenage Dance Hall called the Blue Village. My husband found on eBay 2 CD's of the **THE CRYAN' SHAMES** and we have been enjoying their music over and over as part of our **"way back experience"**! Years ago my husband introduced me to the lead singer when we were dating because they worked together at the golf course. The Blue Village was only open for 2 1/2 years but they my dancing years! I have fond memories of the black neon lights and dancing to the music of the Cryan Shames. I went as often as I could and danced every song! My Dad used to tease me that it was a "crying shame" when I had a a test to study for and couldn't go.

My husband has brought back to the music and dance of my youth & we are singing along with the Cryan Shames.

Wedding Wishes

When passion and commitment come from your Heart, a special bond of trust forms from the start. Always think of your love as a gift that you give to One another.

**Treasure that gift
and mingle in kindness.**

Ask God for guidance as you walk together.

He will be with you in all kinds of weather.

I said "YES"

The day my husband proposed is etched into my heart.

Our courtship had a magical Start!

We had left the dance floor for a quiet spot to talk. The man that I loved had a familiar smile, I wondered if this would be the moment? Did he have the ring? Here I was dancing and now I wanted to sing this man I truly loved and I wanted to sing! Oh, how I longed for this day! Then his quiet and loving way he asked the question and I said *"yes"*!

We both made a committment that day and everyday since. It was a tender moment, a defining moment of my life. Perhaps you have one too?

THE GIFTS OF PARKINSON'S

You may find it odd that I have received gifts for my new adventure with even before I was diagnosed. The chance meeting of my Uncle at a luncheon I was serving was all part of the Shepherd's plan. He was in the later stage of the disease and mentored me in the beginning. We prayed for each other and I shared my poems and we helpd wach other. He was a man of faith and a gift to his family but an inspiration to me .

My Husband has been my life time gift but somhow it he has saved the best for last. Michael J Fox went back in time and we have gone in the "way back machine"reminising our journey from the start.
One morning he greeted me with tunes from the **CRYAN SHAMES** along with my daily dose of prunes calling it "tunes &prunes!"
He has been patient, encouraging, acceptinn and humorous.
My family have all read Michael J. Fox's Book and have been so supportive. There was the PD Doctor who was a
movement Specialist who gave me hope .There was the loss of smell heightened awareness of the other senses. The people that have come into my life old friends and ew friends each with their own unique brand of giving and caring. All have been gifts that have given me
· laughter and joy and made my goood days better and my hard ones easier. A special gits that truely came to me beause of PD are the gal who ran the Parkinson's group. We met and conneted as if wwe had known each oher for a long time, The is the group we have met for coffee aftee we aawlk the mall in the morning. athe grouo keep epanding but this group are all people that are a blessing to have in your life. Salt of the earth genuine people who we consider special friends and they came into our lives as a couple because we walked the mall. This is why I know that the Shepherd is guiding my journey. The first poem written has also been a gift that has toched people of different ages. I have a note from a 1 yr old and a teennsger who is the granddaighter of my friend. I gave her the poem after her skiccident and she wrote a sweet note that made me cry. I have gotten reviews from old friends and strabgers and one from someome I had brifly met and had been moved spiritually by the word in The Messy Bits of life poem. Parkinsn's has brought me back to writing and this books rpreents the hope and prayer I had at the library when I was moved by the words of different poets. I had hoped back then that someday i might find the words that could bring about emotion. My work is vey simple I do not have what great authit=rs have but I believe my little book has brought on emotions and for that it is the answer to a long ago prayer. ONE THING I MUST BE CLEAR ABOUT, MY WORDS ARE JUST THE INSTRUMENT.

It is the AMAZING POWER OF PRAYER and THE LOVE THAT THE CREATOR HAS FOR YOU THAT BRINGS REFLECTION AND EMOTION. It is HIS VOICE, not mine, THAT IS CALLING YOU!

PLANTING SEEDS

We
all have planted seeds that didn't grow for various reasons.
Perhaps they were not watered or planted in
poor soil with too little or too much sunshine? *If a
seed needs attention to grow, just think of all of the
needs that one person has during the course of their lifetime.* Just think of the endless ways you could be
the one making a difference in someone's life. If
we are present in the moment and engaged, than
We are able to see the needs of others and respond.
My husband has captured the message of being
connected in this world of electronics. I am honored
and proud to share his poem in my book. We have
had a strong connection from the very
beginning and God's blessings have been many!

Gather Without the Phone

Face to face is the best place
To enjoy the human face.

Emotions are transmitted
By sights and sounds.

We connect in each other's presence

To be close is to share in our humanity
We can share more than we know
By just being there

Strive to be close without
Distractions

Each moment brings connections
That only comes with human contact.

Written by my husband
Richard Kirkwood M.S.

We found this lantern on our

honeymoon in Wisconsin.

The Old Chicago Lantern

The lanterns of the past
Used kerosene or oil from the whale.
The lantern that inspired this poem we
Bought at a garage sale!
When electricity and gas came along, our
Homes became climate controlled.
We depend on light and find it hard
To do without power for our electronics.
Today the lanterns have LED light.
The lanterns are safe and the beam is very bright.
Keep a lantern handy
So you are ready if the power goes out.
When the kids complain that they
Can't use their electronics or watch TV,
Bring out your lantern
And do what families did long ago.
Tell stories, play charades, puzzles or card games.
Being creative is quite easily done.
Some of the best family memories
Come from "unplanned events"
That families turned into fun!

The waves will challenge you,

but you will find the strength.

Trust in God's plan and

He will lead you to safety.

Unknown Water

Life is fragile, you are lost, but will be
Found. Your faith will carry you through
The unknown water.

The Lord God will bring you to safe
Ground. He will help, but you must
Try, for there is no room for laziness
When you take this ride! Show up, be
Engaged and go with the tide.
When
Life gets bumpy as it often will do, these
Are things that you should try to pursue.
Keep the wind at your back. Keep
Your memories in tack.
Go forward, don't go back
Yesterday is gone and tomorrow will
Be. ALL you have is today.

Live today fully and Completely!

You are much stronger then you think!

When you are healthy

and not in pain,

pray for others who are.

Pain

Many people are visited by pain. You
Never ask for it, but it is a part of life just
The same. Pain can accompany you
On your journey and stay for a short time
Or it can be chronic and intense and can
Linger for a long while. It doesn't matter
If the duration is long or short, pain
Disrupts life and keeps you up at night.
Pain zaps your energy and appears on
Your face and will break through a smile.
Pain can be physical or emotional and
It can be both. It can be the result of
Stress, accident, injury, disease, toxic
Workplace, or a broken relationship.
Pain can be both simple and complex
Such as a task being a pain in the
Neck, a toothache and even a tiny sliver
Can cause pain. When you have pain
It is hard to focus and hard to pray.
The Shepherd understands pain.
He will stay with you.

**Tea parties are always
fun no matter what age!**

A Tea Party Shower

Home is where your story begins and
Where your heart will always lead.
You shall be a Family with a new baby
to feed.
Remember the tea parties when you
Were a little girl?
Remember your favorite dress
That you liked to spin?
Remember playing a game and
Wanting to win?
You made cookies with your mom
And helped make bread, but
You didn't like getting ready for bed!
All of your childhood memories matter,
Because now you will be the Mom
Planning the picnics, the tea parties,
The trips to the park and the zoo.
You will be making the memories for
Your little girl and a lifetime of adventure
Awaits you!

50 years of pumpkin bread

replaced one year with suet!

It's always fun to surprise

The Gift of Seed

Once upon a Christmas
A gal had a silly idea, instead
Of sending Christmas cards, she'd write a
Little poem.
And instead of baking Pumpkin
Bread, she would send the gift
Of seed.

So, open up the package and
You will find a block of suet.
I can almost see you smiling,
For you didn't think I'd do it!

50 years of Christmas bread, and
This year a block of suet!
Hang it on a Shepherd's hook.
Go ahead and do it!

The birds will come to perch and eat.
Bird watching will be your gift
And that is a
Winter's treat!

Nancy Kirkwood   45

The garden is where patience is born.

Bloom

The garden is where patience is
Born. It starts with a little seed and
You wait for that seed to sprout.
Planting and waiting are what
Living is all about!
The sun shines and the rain will fall.
The plant begins to grow quite tall.
Discovering our gifts is an
Ongoing process.
We rise and we fall and our mistakes
We must address. The Shepherd
Is always there.
He calls and He will wait.
He forgives and it's never too late.
He knows when we are in distress.
If you are seeking the light, look
Within for His light is already there.
Let Christ into your life,
Give Him room.
You will Blossom, you will
Bloom!

Zero Birthdays

Oh, those zero birthdays come so fast
At nine you couldn't wait for
"10" to come around at last!
Each decade since brings pause and
Some reflection that time alone
Will teach, but none more
Precious than family and friends
Who are right within your reach.
A friend can make a difference
Simply by being there. You have
Been that kind of friend, a
Treasure because you care. So
Many blessings can be counted,
Far more than struggles it's true.
May the Holy Spirit continue to
Guide you on the path that was
Meant for you. I'm glad that
Our paths have crossed.

Happy Birthday!

Ribbons and Bows

Inside this basket is an assortment
Of ribbons and bows
When you will need them nobody knows.
Birthdays and other celebrations
Come every year
You may have wrapping paper
Or you may not
But at least your gift will have a pretty bow
To place on the top.

Breakfast for Dinner

Here are some brunch recipes
That will serve two or twenty-two.
They are the best from all the rest
And they've been put to the test!
How about serving breakfast for dinner?
The family will vote this to be a winner.
Life is all about changes, adapting as we go.
So having breakfast for dinner
Gives the cook a break and goes with
Life's flow!

These are the giving hands
of my Granddaughter

When my children were small
I tried to teach them
that" sharing is caring".

It works sometimes!

Giving

A happy person is one that freely gives.
The giver reaches out of themselves
Seeking nothing in return.
Ironically, the giver often feels that they
Received more than they gave.
This is why the greatest gift you can give
To another is to love them!
"Giving" and "Doing" are the actions of
A selfless person. Greed and the desire for
Success at any cost produces
Self-centered people. If money is your
Goal you have missed the boat and
You will never have enough and always
Want more.
You have been loved first by God and
His love has no beginning and no end
And will always *be* even if human love
Falls short.
When we truly Love, we want to Give!

We never stand alone.

No Flower Stands Alone

No flower stands alone
For the garden's beauty
Is in the design.
Each flower complements another.
We are like the flowers for we do not
Stand alone.
God has planted us exactly
Where we should be.

His design is for us to grow and
Flourish. In the garden of life, we need
To help one another.
We are given
Many opportunities to sow seeds of
Hope and Love.
We can make a difference
When we care.

Whatever challenges you face,
The Lord is always with you.
You will never stand alone.

Live Life Completely

Perhaps you've heard the saying that if you want to see God smile, tell Him your plans!
If that's true, then God must be smiling at me all the time. You see I'm a planner, it's part of who I am. Planning was a necessary tool in raising five active and fiercely independent children. Planning meals, activities, sporting events, doctor visits, and birthday parties, was my speciality. We never stopped moving and I was blessed with boundless energy back when I needed it the most. God was there when my plans came together, **and He was there when "His plan" was different than mine!**

You see, God's plan for us is always the best plan

For He knows us better than we know ourselves.

I decided that I wasn't going to let Parkinson's define me. I simply would adjust and continue with life, appreciating the good days and dealing with the ones that weren't. I was at peace, but God had more plans that came very unexpectedly one morning after our daily walk at the mall. I was tired and thought I'd take a nap. As I headed up the stairs I was out of breath **and once again God was there. He gave me a clear sign, no pain but a strange feeling that something was wrong!**
We got back in the car and went to the emergency room to check it out. I took two crushed aspirins just in case it was heart related. My husband got me to the emergency room door and went to park the carI was attended to ASAP!

My heart attack began in the emergency room.

If you're going to have a Heart Attack
the ER is not a bad place to be!
I had 95% blockage in a major artery (The RCA)
And a stent was put in the artery to allow the blood to
flow in record speed. I had no pain or radiation down
my arm so I could have just as easily gone to bed
and would have had the heart attack at home in my sleep.

I went through the cardiac rehab and eight months
later I noticed my blood pressure was staying higher
then it had been. The doctor ordered a stress test
and the other major artery (the LAD) was
90% blocked. I was back to operating room immediately
and two more stents were out in placed just
In time to avoid a second heart attack.
The artery they fixed is called the "widow maker".
I came dangerously close to death twice
which leaves a person keenly aware of
how fragile life is! None of us knows the
time or the place when the Lord will call us home.
He calls the young and He calls the old.
**Our time on Earth is short
compared to eternity.**
Live today fully and completely
and live in the light of the Lord.
Let Him in, open the door and
**TRUST IN "HIS PLAN" EVEN
IF I DIFFERS FROM YOURS!**

DANCE IN THE LIGHT

We dance in the light of each new day,
We celebrate together, we listen,
We pray.
Our stories are different,
Our journey's aren't the same
But the Shepherd loves us all
And He calls out our name.
The path that we take
Is the choice that we make.
If you choose to follow
He will be there in all of your joys
and all of your sorrow.
He will be with you today,
as well as tomorrow.
He is your forever friend
and will never leave.
Open your heat
TODAY
and just
BELIEVE!

LOST AN FOUND

I hoped that my words could
be an instrument of peace.
A song of joy, a melody to share
I asked for courage to be more aware.
I wanted to reach the young and the old
to be simple and maybe a bit bold.
To call out to those who were lost in the fold.
To bring hope and perhaps plant a seed
For God sent me a gift when I had a need.
Some things are lost and others are found
Building your house needs solid ground.
If we are to dance we must first need to walk
And it can be a struggle for some people to talk.
Everything has a time and a place,
and life unfolds slowly it isn't a race.
Some things are lost forever it may seem
and then you remember in a dream.
The poems of my Youth were shredded indeed
But the titles of two have made their debut
The Senior versions are surely not the same,
But a lifetime of experience will always remain.

" Unique" is the Re-write of the
Lost Poem of my youth

This was a gift from my husband.

My son proudly built the stand. The wheels spin in
the wind.

It's a unique garden piece of art.

Unique

We are all uniquely and wonderfully made
With gifts that need to be shared

It is our differences that challenenges
Find common ground

Listening, accepting, and
Understanding is all needed for the
Bond of love to be found.

So, bring your uniqueness, your personal style
To each day of the week.

Be Bold.
Be Kind.
Be Humble.
Be Loving and meek.But most of all
be Aware of God's presence
working in your life.

tapestry is a re-write of the lost poem from my youth

This beautiful quilt was

made by my friend

Kathleen Durochik who is also a neighbor.

Tapestry

We are all part of the same cloth of humanity
The complexity of the weave is a design so
Intricate that it could only be created by God's
very hands.

In His design many gifts were given
And the gifts were meant to be shared.

The cloth is stitched with both
Common and uncommon threads. Each
Uniquely different, yet connected.
The threads are multi colored
and the colors are as
Brilliant as found in nature.

We see the backside of the cloth with all the
Loose and unfinished ends.
We are a work in progress!

The Creator sees the best that we can be.
He sees what we can hope to achieve.
Listen for His call.
Ask for strength in adversity
And trust in His plan
As it unfolds.

When you shop

be careful and be smart.

The Cart

Many things in life involve
The use of a cart.
Whether you're at the grocery store
Or the mall, some items that you need
Are large and some are small.
You might
Even shop online and put your items
Into a virtual cart!
Whatever way you shop, make careful
Choices and be smart. Fill your cart with
Things you need. Don't get too involved
In collecting more. There is no end to
What you can buy at a given store!
Fill your cart with things that matter.
Fill your life with love!

When it comes to volunteering,

There is a time

to say "YES"

and a time

to say"NO".

Volunteering

When you volunteer it is a job worth
Your effort and your time.
You volunteer by choice, you don't
Complain or whine.

Perhaps you are the person who often
Says *yes*, and find it hard to say *no*?

You are probably called first because
You get the job done and you make it fun!

If volunteering keeps you so busy that
Other things are being neglected, then
It is time to think about saying *no*.

Sometimes volunteering becomes a
Burden and is no longer fun.
This is the time to get up and run!

Everyone who volunteers should
Know that balance is the ultimate
Goal!

Nancy Kirkwood **65**

Comfortable clothes,

comfort food and

spending time with a friend

PRICELESS!

Caftans and Casseroles

A caftan is a gift that is unique,
It is comfortable,
It will fit in your suitcase
And will fold up small.

You probably don't have one in your closet
And you won't find it at the mall.

I hope you do enjoy.
Humor me with this I do employ. This
Roomy *caftan* is the perfect thing to
Wear on your day off,
But you can't wear it to play golf.

Please wear your new caftan
Once in a while,
Who cares if it is or isn't in style!

Be a person who sends out good vibrations.

Good Vibrations

Some people just make you feel happy.
They draw you in and leave good vibrations!
These friends are easy to
Make and easy to keep.
I learned long ago that it is important to
Also get to know people who are difficult.
These are the people that it takes effort
Just to say hello.
When you look behind the crusty shell,
There is often something that you missed,
Maybe you judged and just dismissed.
That person may be carrying a heavy
Burden that you never knew,
Because you never asked.
When we stop and listen, we accept.
When we walk away, we reject.
You can't make everyone happy, but a
Little kindness can brighten anyone's
Day. Be a person who sends out
Good vibrations!

If you have a choice
Choose to dance!

**These are my Granddaughter's
dancing feet**

Dance

Dance, Dance, Dance!
I am happy when I dance.
It is the music that sets me free.
When I dance, I forget that I have PD.
I stumble when I walk, and I mumble
When I talk. Parkinson's makes my
Body stiff you see, but when I dance I
Am loose, the music flows through me.
This room was full of strangers, but now
We're kindred spirits floating about with
Glee.
The dance is the connection,
Each step is the best we can be. The
People we meet on this journey help us
To go with the flow. The dance
Is the link and
The Lord of the dance
Is in control.

He takes the lead.
We simply follow, letting Him intercede.

Reunions and memories of the past.

Class Reunion

Reunions bring back memories, when
Our life's story had just begun.
The process of growing up is mixed
With drama, intensity and fun.

All of our
Experiences build in ways that we
Often aren't aware. Connecting with
Old friends reminds us that each person
Who has touched our lives made a
Difference because they were there!

50 Years later we value each day as a gift.

Each friend is a treasure!
There is a common thread that has
Brought us this far and God's love
That has carried us to the place
That we now are.

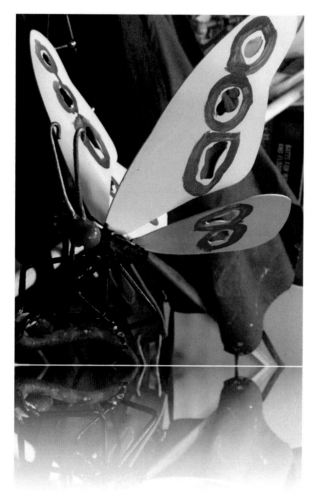

This poem doesn't have a hidden message.

This one is just for fun!

Ode to Regular

How do you keep your system in
Sync? Eat more fiber and get lots to
Drink!

So, if you have the need
To move, prunes and apricots will get you
In the groove.

Beans work well in chili or soup,
But be careful
Too much will make you toot!

Perhaps this all is a bit of
Oversharing

But sometimes things get tied up and
Can be a bit overbearing!

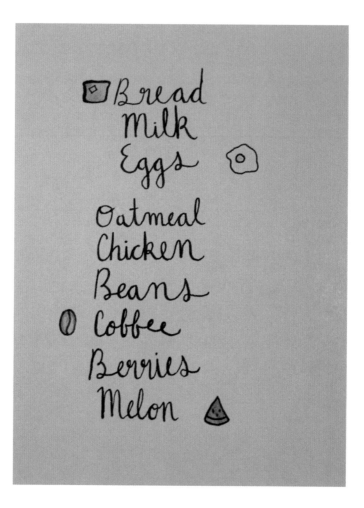

Bread
Milk
Eggs

Oatmeal
Chicken
Beans
Coffee
Berries
Melon

The List

I wish that I could find my list.
There must be something on it
That I have missed.

I have to laugh at myself.
Because when my list is found,
I can't read it because my
Glasses
Have dropped
To the ground!

They say these are everyday
Happenings for people
Of a certain age?

Sometimes I'm hot, and
Sometimes I'm cold.

But when you get
Right down to it,
I'm just getting old!

Choosing a path. We all make choices.
Some are good and some are not,
but we can always re-evaluate
and change directions.
We can only move forward
and learn from our mistakes.

Taking Chances

It's good to take a chance.
Trust your instincts,
Never judge,
Search deeper than first glance.

Speak your opinion,
But let your actions match your word.
It's as important to listen to others, as
Well as to let your voice be heard.

There are two sides to every opinion, and
No one has to be right.
Communication is conversation,
And it doesn't have to be a fight.

You can agree to disagree!
In this era of instant messages,
Emails and tweets
The art of true conversation must be taught.

Take a chance on someone today.
Listen to what they really have to say.

I have fond memories sitting on
my front stairs with my Dad on
A clear night watching the stars.
These kinds of things are
"Spirit filled" Moments.

Little Star

Twinkle, twinkle little star,
Oh, how I wonder who you are?

Soon you will be bringing
Your new baby
Home in your car.

A husband is now a father
And a mother is his wife.

You were just two you see,
Now baby makes three
And now you are a *family*.

When baby wakes and you see
The stars above
Don't forget to thank the Lord
For the sweet baby
That you love!

Parenting is an awesome gift!

For the New Parents

Planted deep in your love story
It seems, is the hand of the Creator
Guiding all of your dreams.

Soon a
New chapter will unfold and a sweet
Baby you will hold.
May the time pass
Quickly as you prepare.
While you wait these things are good to
Think about and be aware.

Your baby will learn all about
Love from the two of you. Being a
Parent is an awesome gift, but it is a big
Responsibility too!

Love your child
As the Lord loves you.
Ask for this guidance and He will bless
You.

God sometimes places us

in difficult places.

When dealing with a challenge

ask for His help and

He will give you the strength

to do what is best.

Be brave and listen when He calls.

Navigating Loneliness

Loneliness is a very strong emotion. It is
A state of mind, a moment in time.
Loneliness can be turned around
If a friend is there, a friend who is aware.

Sometimes the lonely person hides and
Becomes isolated living in fear. This is
When a good friend is so dear.
If depression becomes intense
and the duration persists, some
kind soul must not delay.
This is not an easy task and
the depressed person Doesn't always ask.
If you are aware and you see, Then
God has put you there
For you are the one to care.
Bring hope, bring light where darkness lives.
There are many ways a person gives.
**Remember, it only takes a pinhole of light
To see in a dark tunnel.**
Help navigate loneliness before
depression sets in.
Be the light that breaks through the fog.
Be the one Holding the lantern!

This was my granddaughter's first rainbow!

She was so excited and wanted to

call her Nana and tell me all about it.

The wonder and joy in her voice was so clear.

This was a spirit-filled moment.

I was sure of it when she said

"We should pray"!

She was just 3 yrs old

The Good Stuff

There is always time enough for the
Important things!
The balance can be challenging, but
When there is a will, there is
Always a way.

All we need to do is the best that we can
With each day that we are given.
There is no perfection
In being human!
There is always lots of room for improvement!
God sends us all kinds of
"Spirit filled moments" to lift us up and let
Us know He is there.

They come to us when
One person touches the soul of another.
This is how we can be an
Instrument of ***His peace.***
When love abides - God resides!
We are all connected in the
Tapestry of life.

We are never too young
or
too old to begin to pray

These are my youngest grandson's praying hands

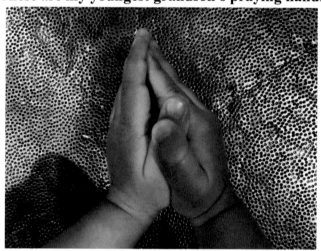

Prayer matters!

THE EASTER MESSAGE

He came with words of hope and love
Into our world from above.
He came for the young
and He came for the old.
He came for the lonely and depressed.
He came for the poor and the well dressed.
He came for the arrogant & the meek,
He came for the strong & the weak.
He came for the haves and the have nots.
He came for the lazy and the ambitious
Jesus sacrifice on the Cross
Was for all of us for our sins.
It is through Jesus that we come to
know the Father.
So let us all be Easter people
Fill your heart with joy,
Sing and dance with the Risen Lord
Look for the Spirit filled moments and
bear your cross, whatever it may be.
The Holy Spirit will guide you and Peace He will
leave with thee.

One Moment in Time
Time passes by so quickly
Oh how the time goes by!
Day by day and year by year
There is your time and my time,
Family time, alone time and
The time we have right now!
It takes time for a seed to germinate.
It takes time for a flower to bloom,
It takes time for a baby to grow in a
Mother's womb.
It takes time to grow a friend
It takes time for fences to mend
So
Take the time to know the Maker of light
The Creator of all the day and the night.
Prayer changes things
and requires just a little time.
So, when you go about your day,
Stop for a moment now and then
And take the time to pray.

May your roots
Go down deep
Into the soil
Of God's marvelous love.
EPHESIANS 3:17

ABOUT THE AUTHOR

Nancy is married to Rich Kirkwood and they 5 children

two boys and three girls. Four are married and they have

one daughter-in-law, 3 sons-in-law and 9 grandchildren.

One adult son lives at home. Nancy is a Registered Nurse. Throughout the years she has volunteered her time in varies capacities at her Church often taking leadership roles,, teaching and serving meals. She has helped families using her nursing skills and worked blood drives. She and her husband have worked together their entire married life. Nancy is an avid gardener and a member of The Daisy Garden Club. Through the years she has enjoyed hosting parties especially "theme parties" & soup and salad lunches. She loves music and dance, poetry and a warm Irish Scone. If you are her friend you probably have something she a has laminated for you. It might be a poem or one of her favorite recipes. She has been known to wear out laminating machines and garden gloves. She loves Cherries in the season and frozen grapes!Recently she & her husband celebrated their 49h Wedding Anniversary with a psrty for family and friends. The party ended with a rainbow that filled the sky from one end to the other.

The Rainbow was a special gift

because the couple had a rainbow

on their wedding day!

Nancy feels that God sends "Spirit filled moments" to all of us, but we have to be present in the moment or else we miss them. She hopes that her poems and reflections reach her readers in such a way that they too will see God's presence working in their lives. She hopes to inspire people to trust in God's plan and celebrate life! This couple bids thee Shalom. May you have a good day and a better one tomorrow!.

This was the rainbow at the end of Fun party.

Made in the
USA
Monee, IL